ABORTION: A BIBLICAL CONSIDERATION

By

SANDRA SWEENY SILVER

1stBooks - rev. 03/20/02

TABLE OF CONTENTS

INTRODUCTION

Until the latter half of the twentieth century, the world has NEVER embarked upon open, systematic, government-sponsored, wholesale slaughter of babies within the womb. Each year uncountable millions of children are torn from the stomachs of women in America, Africa, Europe, Russia, China, Japan, India, everywhere. No continent or country is immune from the practice or innocent of the blood.

The central premise of this book is: Abortion, the killing of a baby in the womb, is contrary to Biblical teaching.

One of the most effective ways to fight this world policy of abortion is with the powerful, consuming, convicting, never-futilely-used Word of God.

The Bible Verses and Consideration which follow are first of all provided for those who are actively engaged in the fight to end abortion. They are reinforcements for this valiant army.

Secondly, there are many who are on the side lines watching the changing fortunes of this battle. Some are confused or uninformed. They may feel abortion is wrong, but arguments appear so persuasive. They don't have the time or inclination to reason and to research all the rhetoric to a conclusion. Many Bible-believing Jews and Christians are perhaps in this category. This book hopes to give all side-liners the Scriptures they need to make a choice.

Finally, this book is written for those who are For Abortion. It displays the arsenal of God arrayed against them so that they may know exactly what and with Whom they are really fighting. This Consideration offers them amnesty and redemption if they will turn away from these murders.

Some of you may not believe the Bible is the Word of God to man. By reading this Consideration, you will at the very least be exposed to the considerable amount of historically-venerated scriptures which speak clearly for the holiness and sanctity of life within the womb.

"(Roe Versus Wade) contradicts the acknowledged precepts of the Christian religion. It violates the noblest instincts of humanity; it asks us to trample on the Law of God. It commands what nature, religion and God alike forbid; it forbids what nature, religion and God alike command."

Said by Theodore Parker, a Boston Congregational minister, in 1851 about The Fugitive Slave Law.

OWNERSHIP

ACCORDING TO THE BIBLE, THE BABY IN THE WOMB IS GOD'S CREATION. GOD, NOT WOMAN, "OWNS" THE PRE-NATAL CHILD.

PSALM 139:13-16

"You created every part of me; You put me together in my mother's womb. I praise You because You are to be feared; all You do is strange and wonderful. I know it with all my heart. When my bones were being formed, carefully put together in my mother's womb, when I was growing there in secret, You knew I was there—You saw me before I was born. The days allotted to me had all been recorded in Your book, before any of them ever began."

ECCLESIASTES 11: 5

"As you do not know how the spirit comes to the bones in the womb of a woman with child, so you do not know the work of God Who makes everything."

ACTS 17: 24-28

"God, Who made the world and everything in it, is Lord of heaven and earth and does not live in man-made temples. Nor does He need anything that we can supply by working for Him, since it is He Himself Who gives life and breath and everything else to everyone. From one man He created all races of

1

mankind and made them live throughout the whole earth. He Himself fixed beforehand the exact times and limits of the places where they would live. He did this so that they would look for Him, and perhaps find Him as they felt around for Him. Yet God is actually not far from any of us; as someone has said, In Him we live and move and exist. It is as some of your poets have said, we too are His children."

ISAIAH 44: 2, 24

"Thus says the Lord Who made you, Who formed you from the womb and will help you...Thus says the Lord, your Redeemer, Who formed you from the womb."

JOB 10: 8-12

"Your hands formed and shaped me, and now those same hands destroy me. Remember that You made me from clay; are You going to crush me back to dust? You gave my father strength to beget me; You made me grow in my mother's womb. You formed my body with bones and sinews and covered the bones with muscles and skin. You have given me life and constant love, and Your care has kept me alive."

DEUTERONOMY 14:1

"You are the children of the Lord, your God."

ISAIAH 66: 9

"Shall I bring to the birth and not cause to bring forth? says the Lord; <u>shall I, Who cause to bring forth,</u> shut the womb? says your God."

PSALM 100: 3

"Know that the Lord is God. <u>It is He Who made us and we are His;</u> we are His people, the sheep of His pasture."

JAMES 1: 16-18

"Do not be deceived, my beloved brethren. Every good endowment and every perfect gift is from above, coming down from the Father of Lights with Whom there is no variation or shadow due to change. <u>Of His Own will He brought us forth by the word of truth that we should be a kind of first fruits of His creatures.</u>"

DEUTERONOMY 32: 18

"You were unmindful of the rock that begot you, and <u>you forgot the God Who gave you birth.</u>"

GENESIS 29: 31, 32

"When the Lord saw that Leah was hated, <u>He opened her womb;</u> but Rachel was barren. And Leah conceived and bore a son, and she called his name Reuben; for she said, Because the Lord has looked upon my affliction; surely now my husband will love me."

GENESIS 30: 22-24

"Then God remembered Rachel, and <u>God hearkened to her and opened her womb.</u> She conceived and bore a son, and said, God has taken away my reproach; and she called his name Joseph, saying, May the Lord add to me another son!"

RUTH 4: 11-13, 17

"Then all the people who were at the gate, and the elders said, We are witnesses. May the Lord make the woman who is coming into your house like Rachel and Leah, who together built up the house of Israel. May you prosper in Ephrathah and be renowned in Bethlehem; and may your house be like the house of Perez; whom Tamar bore to Judah, <u>because of the children that the Lord will give you by this young woman.</u> So Boaz took Ruth and she became his wife; and he went in to her, and <u>the Lord gave her conception, and she bore a son</u>…They named him Obed; he was the father of Jesse, the father of David."

ISAIAH 64: 8

"<u>Yet, O Lord, Thou art our Father, we are the clay, and Thou art our potter; we are all the work of Thy hand.</u>"

MALACHI 2: 10

"Have we not all one Father? Has not one God created us all? Why then are we faithless to one another, profaning the covenant of our fathers?"

JOB 31: 15

"Did not He Who made me in the womb make them? Did not the same One form us both within our mothers?"

PSALM 119: 73

"Thy hands have made and fashioned me; give me understanding that I may learn Thy commandments."

ISAIAH 51: 13

"Have you forgotten the Lord Who made you?"

ECCLESIASTES 12: 1-7

"Remember also your Creator in the days of your youth,
Before the evil days come, and the years draw nigh, when you will say, I have no pleasure in them,
Before the sun and the light and the moon and the stars are darkened and the clouds return after the rain;

In the day when the keepers of the house tremble, and the strong men are bent, and the grinders cease because they are few,

And those that look through the windows are dimmed, and the doors on the street are shut;

When the sound of the grinding is low, and one rises up at the voice of a bird, and all the daughters of song are brought low;

They are afraid also of what is high, and terrors are in the way;

The almond tree blossoms, the grasshopper drags itself along and desire fails;

Because man goes to his eternal home, and the mourners go about the streets;

Before the silver cord is snapped, or the golden bowl is broken, or the pitcher is broken at the fountain,

Or the wheel broken at the cistern,

And the dust returns to the earth as it was,

And the spirit returns to God Who gave it."

ISAIAH 8: 18

"Behold, <u>I and the children whom the Lord has given me</u> are signs and portents..."

JOB 33: 3, 4

"All my words are sincere, and I am speaking the truth. <u>God's Spirit made me and gave me life.</u>"

When the Father answers Job out of the whirlwind, He reveals Himself as not only Creator General but Minute Overseer of all particulars of creation.

"Where were you when I laid the foundation of the earth? Who determined its measurements...On what were its bases sunk, or who laid its cornerstone?" Job 38:4-6

"Where is the way to the dwelling of light, and where is the place of darkness?" Job 38:19

"What is the way to the place where the light is distributed, or where the east wind is scattered upon the earth?" Job 38:24

"Has the rain a father, or who has begotten the drops of dew? From whose womb did the ice come forth, and who has given birth to the hoarfrost of heaven?" Job 38:28, 29

"Can you bind the chains of the Pleiades, or loose the cords of Orion? Can you lead forth the Mazzaroth in their season, or can you guide the Bear with its children? Do you know the ordinances of the heavens? Can you establish their rule on the earth?" Job 38:31-33

"Who can number the clouds by wisdom?" Job 38:37

"Do you observe the calving of hinds?" Job 39:1

"Is it by your wisdom that the hawk soars, and spreads his wings toward the south?" Job 39:26

"Who provides for the raven its prey, when its young ones cry to God, and wander about for lack of food?" Job 38:41

At the end of these descriptions of just a few aspects of His creation and control, God asks Job, "Shall he that contends with the Almighty instruct Him?" (Job 40:2)

The rhetorical questions the Creator asked Job are as unfathomed today as they were when our brother Job underwent his Divine grilling. But the ultimate answer to all these timeless questions is the same now as it was then. God did it all. God is the Creator. In our quest we ultimately bump into the Father.

We are reminded in the Job passage that it is our Creator Who put wisdom deep within us and has given us hearts capable of understanding. (Job 38:36) God never gives without a purpose. We are to use these critical and sensitive faculties to search out His creation. We are created to pour over, explore, question, cogitate, turn upside down and inside out all the aspects of God's creation.

The more we study and know, the greater should be our appreciation of the Creator.

To describe the infinite patterns of the snowflake, to know the exact temperature and conditions when water becomes snow, to observe specific clouds filled with snow, to parse elements within each flake does not answer the question—Whence snow? To say the words, "Big Bang", does not explain the origin of the gases and elements which had to be there to go "Bang."

But because we cannot answer the question, Why snow?, does not mean we stop searching snow. Because we may never know the exact time and method of universal creation does not mean we cease inquiry.

There is a tantalizing verse in Proverbs 25:2: "It is the glory of God to conceal a thing."

The man who brought me to the Lord, Francis Schaeffer, used to say, "We can never know God completely, but we can know him truly."

"The secret things belong to the Lord our God: but the things that are revealed belong to us and to our children for ever..." (Deuteronomy 29:29)

Those things which are revealed belong to us. We are to appropriate them. We are to cherish them. We are to understand them. We are to use all things, as Bach says of music, "for the permissible delectation of the spirit...and the recreation of the mind."

And in all things we are to give God the glory as Bach did. This is not a hard thing to do. Anyone, believer or unbeliever, who has ever pushed into any facet of creation knows there is a place where man cannot go. We may ascend the stars at the speed of light, but we will never know Why light? Whence movement?

The secret, ultimate things belong to the Creator. But concealed within each part of His creation, within each grain of sand, each star, each atom, each baby is His glory revealed.

It is an easy thing for a sensitive, reasonable person to be humbled by a honeybee much less the gugals of galaxies and the curve of space itself. Because we can never know these wonders completely does not abate our quest to know them truly. Because our children will never be known to us completely does not abate our desire to know them truly. A reasonable person accepts reasonable limitations, is even made modest by them.

For it is in the quest, in the search, in the unfolding play of hide and seek that God's glory and omnipotence are revealed. The toes of a newborn baby, the unforgiving mathematics of space, a speck of pollen all can bring a sane person to his knees.

It is the progressive discovery of things previously concealed that evokes the awe which is so much a part of God's glory. Behind every thing is some thing else. Within every thing is some thing else. Behind and within some thing else is some thing else. The play has been and will be for man an infinite one. And there is glory at every door.

For the Father Creator is a God of glory. He is the Alpha and Omega of Awe. A person may be deceived into thinking he created the door because he discovered the door. He may believe he has come to the end because he has come to the end of his own abilities. He may imagine he has found everything because he has found something. He may assert he creates life because he hosts life. The wise are not so. They cry with Paul:

"O the depth of the riches and wisdom and knowledge of God! How unsearchable are His judgments and how inscrutable His ways! For who has known the mind of the Lord, or who has been His counselor? Or who has given a gift to Him that he might be repaid? For from Him and through Him and to Him are all things. To Him be the glory forever. Amen." (Romans 11:33-36)

God is the Creator of all life and matter. There is no sidestepping that fact in the Bible. All things are FROM Him, THROUGH Him and TO Him. He is the Beginning of all life, the Perpetuator of all life and the End of all life.

Some may imagine God to be deistic. They may imagine He was the Prime Agent of all creation. He set every thing and one in motion and then retired to watch the great clock tick on. He is there, but He is not actively involved with His creation. The whole ball of wax works on inexorable laws which He first set in perpetual motion.

Those who believe such things have never read God's Word. From the Book of Genesis where the Creator is talking with the first people One to one to the Book of Revelation where the Alpha and Omega talks with John the Apostle, there is an unbroken stream of communications and relationships initiated by the Father. The true God is, mirabile dictu, interested in and actively involved with you and me. If you have not responded to your Father's constant wooing of you through His physical creation or the dictates of your heart or mental reasoning or His Word or others who know Him, it must be very hard to fathom why the Creator of it all would want to have a relationship with you, would care about you.

One of the world's greatest poets, King David, struggled with that same feeling. In one of his songs he says,

> "O Lord, our Lord,
> How majestic is Thy Name in all the earth!
> Thou Whose glory above the heavens is chanted
> By the mouth of babes and infants...
> When I look at Thy heavens, the work of Thy Fingers,
> The moon and stars which Thou hast established;
> What is man that Thou art mindful of him
> And the son of man that Thou dost care for him?" (Psalm 8:1-4)

In his turbulent life David spent many nights alone hiding in the desert from King Saul. Anyone who has contemplated the needlework of the night is boggled by the infinity of it all. How can the God Who made all this be at all concerned about mankind let alone the individual person? David had the same questions some of you may have. Yet David knew God personally and knew God knew him personally. That knowledge weighed against the backdrop of outer space was the source of David's praise.

This infinite capacity of God not only to create but to relate to each minute particular of His creation is beyond creature comprehension.

There are billions of people living in the world today. Billions have preceded us. No one can begin to grapple with the ability to know intimately each person living as well as all those who have ever lived.

God has that ability.

We as created ones are limited. Often we can't recall names of people we've just met. We can't recall everyone we've ever met in our life. No one, except one almost totally bald, knows exactly how many hairs he has on his head.

The mind-boggling assertion of God's Word is that your Father knows how many hairs you have on your head!

"But the very hairs on your head are all numbered." (Matthew 10:30)

The running number of hairs you have on your head are known to your Creator. The hairs on my head and on the head of every one who has ever lived are computed by the One Who created us.

That degree of capacity and care is beyond analysis or analogy. But such scrupulous omniscience to strands of hair does make the Job passage about developing babies more comprehensible.

"...You made me grow in my mother's womb. You formed my body with bones and sinews and covered the bones with muscles and skin. You have given me life and constant love, and Your care has kept me alive." (Job 10:11, 12)

Here the Bible says God not only causes the baby in the womb to develop, but He forms the very bones, muscles, sinews, skin. The Bible says the baby in the womb is God's detailed creation.

"You created every part of me; You put me together in my mother's womb." (Psalm 139:13)

"Thy Hands have made and fashioned me." (Psalm 119:73)

The overwhelming testimony of the Bible is that God fashions, God creates the baby in the womb. God is the creator of womb life.

Some will think such a thing preposterous. They will say, The baby in the womb is MY baby. I can do with him or her what I will. If I will to carry this baby to term, I will. If I will to have him or her killed, I will.

The millions who think this way mistakenly believe they created that baby. Thus they are led to believe that they can destroy that baby in the same way and under the same rights that an artist can destroy a painting which doesn't please her or a writer can trash a story which isn't going well.

We are free to believe such things, of course, but we should know full well that we are squared off against God Himself. We should know that the Bible says the baby in the womb is not our PROPERTY to do with what we will. That baby is God's creation— not the possession of the woman and man whose bodies were used to bear that child.

If a human being is the result of a consecrated or an unconsecrated sex act, that human being has God-given life and the right to life which are not ours to cancel. No matter what the circumstances, we are to consider the fruit of the womb holy, God-made.

We are not to consider babies in the womb disposable at whim. We are not to consider babies in the womb bits and pieces which we have somehow pasted together. We are not to consider babies in the womb the result of our own conscious or unconscious fashioning.

The entire political/spiritual war about abortion rests upon ownership of the developing baby. In other words, Does the mother whose womb was fashioned to contain new human life "own" the life growing in secret in the womb? For that matter, Does the earth "own" the seeds and fruit she bears within her dark, fertile womb? Does the earth "own" the earth? Does the man "own" the child he fathers by life-engendering sperm? Does the sun "own" the light without which the earth would be a barren orb? Who "owns" the sun?

In our confused history the question of ownership of the fruit of the womb has been alternately assigned to the female or the male depending upon the culture. Throughout the millennia of confusion the sanity of the Word of God has proclaimed that humans don't "own" any thing or any one here on this planet.

"For all the earth is Mine." (Exodus 19:5)

"The land shall not be sold in perpetuity, for the land is Mine; for you are strangers and sojourners with Me." (Leviticus 25:23)

"The earth is the Lord's and the fullness thereof, the world and those who dwell therein." (Psalm 24:1)

"But who am I, and what is my people, that we should be able thus to offer willingly? For all things come from Thee, and of Thy Own have we given Thee." (I Chronicles 29:14)

"For every beast of the forest is Mine, and the cattle on a thousand hills." (Psalm 50:10)

"The silver is Mine, and the gold is Mine, says the Lord of Hosts." (Haggai 2:8)

"If we live, we live to the Lord, and if we die, we die to the Lord; so then, whether we live or whether we die, we are the Lord's." (Romans 14:8)

"Behold, all souls are Mine; the soul of the father as well as the soul of the son is Mine..." (Ezekiel 18:4)

God is the Owner of every thing and every one. We don't "own" any thing or any one. Sane people know that.

If we are not the owners, what is man's role on earth? What is the sane attitude toward our possessions, our bodies, our children and developing babies?

We are to be stewards and we are to have the attitudes and behaviors of good stewards.

The word <u>steward</u> is not used much anymore except in the transportation industries: steward and stewardess on planes, deck steward, cabin steward on ships; steward on trains. It's an Old English word which came to mean a person who oversaw the running of his master's household. The steward of an estate made sure everything and everyone operated the way the owner of the estate had instructed.

God has given us stewardship over the earth and our bodies. We are the keepers of Another's property. The caretaker of an estate is not the owner of the estate. He is the person the rightful owner has empowered to take care of his property. The owner gives instructions to the caretaker regarding what he wants done to maintain the property.

Our instruction book, the Bible, is clear. The earth is the Lord's. You and I are the Lord's. The baby in the womb is the Lord's. Every thing and every one is not its own or his own or her own.

We are owned. We are not owners.

My husband and I are current stewards of a small piece of land which has existed in one fashion or another from the Beginning. In one hundred years our home has had six "owners." If the Lord tarries, it will have others who will temporarily fill its lovely rooms with things and people and memories. We are conscious of the fact that this house and land are not exclusively ours. We are, as the Bible says, sojourners who have made this house a stopping place on our pilgrimage and we will become a part of the pilgrimage of the house itself.

While living here, I have become interested in gardening. I am thankful to some of the previous stewards of the land for excellent shrubs and bushes planted strategically and staggered in bloom. I hope future stewards will enjoy the perennial flower beds I have dug and planted.

Working with the earth has been a joy and a humbling. So many of the principles in the Bible are based on this form of stewardship.

"Behold, A sower went forth to sow..." (Matthew 13:3)

"Consider the lilies of the field..." (Matthew 6:28)

"There was a certain householder, which planted a vineyard." (Matthew 21:33)

"Doth the plowman plow all day to sow? doth he open and break the clods of his ground?" (Isaiah 28:24)

"For they have sown the wind, and they shall reap the whirlwind." (Hosea 8:7)

"A good tree cannot bring forth evil fruit, neither can a corrupt tree bring forth good fruit." (Matthew 7:18)

"The kingdom of heaven is likened unto a man which sowed good seed in his field." (Matthew 13:24)

"Sow to yourselves in righteousness, reap in mercy; break up your fallow ground: for it is time to seek the Lord, till He come and rain righteousness upon you." (Hosea 10:12)

The Bible pins man to the earth. The Scriptures constantly admonish: Look, man, the principles you observe around you parable a reality within you.

The gardener has a pragmatic intuition of the sovereignty of nature which the believer sees as the jot and tittleness of God. Every little thing has importance and great things come from things of small import. Gardeners know seeds and tiny, tiny plants are very important.

This gardener does not pray for her plants, but she does have a rude stone with "God Gives The Increase" painted on it. It is embedded near delphiniums which refuse to conform to picture books and beside astilbes which rival catalogues. I do what I can or have time to do to make all the plants happy. I am frequently disappointed and often delighted. I always feel a sense of poignant irrelevance. Nature has sovereignty. God gives the increase.

I have gardened long enough to know I don't know much about the miracle of growth. I know, however, that if I plant carrot seeds, carrots will come up. If I plant asters, I will not get cosmos. Whatever I sow, I will reap.

No gardener would pretend to know how the mighty oak from the small acorn or how the spreading bed of thyme from those tiny, black seeds. We know it happens, but we do not know how. We know the principles of earth, seed death, germination, water, light. We can describe process and conditions, but we cannot account for the miracle of growth itself.

The potential and power of the seed will ever be beyond our grasp.

We can likewise describe the process and conditions for the development of human seeds, but we cannot reckon with the miracle of growth. We know it happens, but we do not know how the spirit comes to a child in the womb. (Ecclesiastes 11:5) As with all seed, conditions may be maximum, but the seed does not germinate. Conditions may be minimal, but the seed germinates. There is a Will there which man cannot manipulate or coerce with certainty. There is the sovereignty of God the Father. The secret, ultimate things are known only to Him Who created them.

For the diligent steward, the delight far outweighs the disappointment. The garden is a fine place to learn awe and humility.

We are not told specifically in the Bible that God forms and fashions the pistils and stamens of each flower. Given His bent for beauty and His capacity for care, He probably does.

But we are told He forms and fashions each baby in each womb. We act upon and obey that which has been revealed to us as good stewards should. Someday we will know even as we are known. (I Corinthians 13:12)

There are some gardeners who nurture with daily care and watchfulness the emergence of microscopic green spots on brown earth. They rejoice and feel pride in their part of this miracle of growth. Some of these same gardeners with impunity and coldness will spread their legs and have torn out of them a little one who would look like they do and would follow them around the garden with little rakes and would wonder as they do over the infinite miracle of sweet-smelling thyme from a seed of such small consequence. Some gardeners are like that.

Why? Why this schizophrenia among us? Why do ordinary people carefully nurse seedlings and heedlessly annihilate babies? Why do people save stray cats and kill babies? Why do people kill babies so they can continue being magazine editors? Why do people kill babies because they don't have a lot of money? Why do people kill one child and let another child live? Why do not-perfect people kill babies because the babies are not-perfect? Why do people kill babies and then use the babies' brains and cells as spare parts to save other babies' lives? Why do people kill babies and sell them by the pound or bag? Something is very wrong in this angle of the universe.

Many of you who are reading these words are saying, My God, that's insane to do those things! We have lost our sanity all together!

Man has not been sane since the Garden. Our history began in a great deception: God says, Don't do that or else. The deceiver says, God's wrong.

We fell for it.

God says, The fruit of the womb is Mine. We say, God's wrong. God says, I made that baby in the womb. We say, God's wrong. God says, I have a purpose for that child. We say, No, God doesn't. God says, The earth is Mine. We say, No, it isn't. God says, The silver and the gold are Mine. We say, You must be crazy.

21

The progressive descent into insanity ends by calling God a liar. Man becomes arbiter, judge, jury and final authority. Woe to all colors, races and ages of human life when the creature tries to sit on the throne of the Creator of all life. All hell breaks loose. The insane happens.

The creature playing Creator happened in the middle of the 20th century and is happening again right now—every 21 seconds in America a baby is killed in the womb.

How did we come to this place?

All evil, individual or societal, thrives under certain conditions. As in the Beginning, the Lie must be sown and nourished. A 2" petunia is not a petunia. A 2" baby is not a baby. A crumb of bread is not bread.

A 2" baby is not a baby. It is—fetal tissue.

In order to destroy human life with impunity, a person or society must be deceived into thinking human life is not really human. In the practice of abortion, man is deceived by the reduction of human life to a sterile medical phrase. There have been recent times when man has reduced human beings to numbers. It is easier to kill a number or a medical phrase.

But the Lie itself is not enough to germinate such evils. The Lie must be nourished by Authority. In order to have wholesale killing of human beings, the Lie must gradually or suddenly become public policy, party line, medical practice, court-ruled, government-sponsored. Acknowledged, honored experts must foster, push and publish the Lie. They must lend their names, organizations, reputations and research to the Lie. Authority must make the Lie appear to be true.

When the Lie is wedded to Authority, people soon follow. Numbers of people believing and practicing the Lie is the third condition for wholesale evil. The Lie may not at first seem right, but it must be right if the courts, the doctors, the newspapers, organizations and experts say it is right. When great numbers of people buy the Lie, the fringe voices of dissent are viewed as hysterical, reactionary, uncaring, crazy, bigoted, religious fanatics, uneducated, naive. When the Lie gets big enough and Authority gets strong enough, dissent is silenced, drowned out, goes underground or is killed.

The Lie of Abortion is: You are not killing your baby. You are getting rid of fetal tissue. It's not a baby.

The Authority wedded to the Lie is: the Supreme Court, the Congress, occasionally a President, the lower courts and legal system, the medical profession, scientists and researchers, the Feminist Movement.

The Numbers of people believing and practicing the Lie: 1.5 million abortions a year just in America. Plus the aiders and abettors of abortions—the millions of fathers of the babies, the grandmothers and grandfathers of the babies, the friends and counselors of the mothers of the babies and, of course, the doctors who perform the abortions, their nurses, receptionists, etc. and the people who rent them the buildings, supply them the instruments of death. The hordes of people incidental to the abortion industry but who service it in any way are wedded to the Numbers who practice the Lie.

Abortion is contrary to the repeated teachings of the Bible. The Bible says God forms the baby in the womb. That developing child is not the property of the woman who hosts him or her. The baby in the womb is God's creation. Man is not to destroy God's creation.

PURPOSE

ACCORDING TO THE BIBLE, GOD KNOWS AND HAS A PURPOSE FOR EVERY CHILD WHO IS CONCEIVED OR WILL BE CONCEIVED.

ISAIAH 49: 1, 2, 5
    (Isaiah's Pre-Natal Calling and Purpose.)

"Listen to me, distant nations, you people who live far away! Before I (Isaiah) was born, the Lord chose me and appointed me to be His servant. He made my words as sharp as a sword. With His own hand He protected me. He made me like an arrow, sharp and ready for use...Before I was born, the Lord appointed me; He made me his servant to bring back His people, to bring back the scattered people of Israel. The Lord gives me honor; He is the source of my strength."

JEREMIAH 1: 4, 5
    (Jeremiah's Pre-Conception Purpose.)

"Now the word of the Lord came to me (Jeremiah) saying, Before I formed you in the womb I knew you, and before you were born I consecrated you; I appointed you a prophet to the nations."

GALATIANS 1: 15
    (Paul's Pre-Natal Purpose.)

"<u>But God in His grace chose me (Paul) even before I was born,</u> and called me to serve Him."

GENESIS 16: 7-12
(Announcement of Ishmael's Gender and Personality Even Before He Was Born.)

"The angel of the Lord met Hagar at a spring in the desert on the road to Shur and said, Hagar, slave of Sarai, where have you come from and where are you going? She answered, I am running away from my mistress. He said, Go back to her and be her slave. <u>Then He said, I will give you so many descendants that no one will be able to count them. You are going to have a son, and you will name him Ishmael,</u> because the Lord has heard your cry of distress. <u>But your son will be against everyone, and everyone will be against him. He will live apart from his relatives.</u>" (Ishmael was the father of the Arab nations.)

GENESIS 17: 15-22
(Covenant Purpose for Isaac Announced Even Before He Was Conceived)

"God said to Abraham, You must no longer call your wife Sarai; from now on her name is Sarah. I will bless her, and <u>I will give you a son by her. I will bless her, and she will become the mother of nations, and there will be kings among her descendants.</u> Abraham bowed down with his face touching the ground, but he began to laugh when he thought, Can a man have a child when he is a hundred years old? Can Sarah have a child at ninety? He asked God, Why not let

26

Ishmael be my heir? But God said, No. Your wife Sarah will bear you a son and you will name him Isaac. (In Hebrew "Isaac" means "he laughs.") I will keep my covenant with him and with his descendants forever. It is an everlasting covenant. I have heard your request about Ishmael, so I will bless him and give him many children and descendants. He will be the father to twelve princes, and I will make a great nation of his descendants. But I will keep my covenant with your son Isaac, who will be born to Sarah about this time next year. When God finished speaking to Abraham, He left him."

HEBREWS 11: 11, 12

"It was faith that made Abraham able to become a father, even though he was too old and Sarah herself could not have children. He trusted God to keep His promise. Though Abraham was practically dead, from this one man came as many descendants as there are stars in the sky, as many as the numberless grains of sand on the seashore."

GENESIS 25: 19-26
(Pre-Natal Purpose and Personality of Esau and Jacob)

"This is the story of Abraham's son Isaac. Isaac was forty years old when he married Rebecca, the daughter of Bethuel, an Armean from Mesopotamia and sister of Laban. Because Rebecca had no children, Isaac prayed to the Lord for her. The Lord answered his prayer and Rebecca became pregnant.

She was going to have twins, and before they were born, they struggled against each other in her womb. She said, Why should something like this happen to me? So she went to ask the Lord for an answer. <u>The Lord said to her, Two nations are within you; You will give birth to two rival peoples. One will be stronger than the other; The older will serve the younger.</u> The time came for her to give birth, and she had twin sons. The first one was reddish, and his skin was like a hairy robe, so he was named Esau. The second one was born holding tightly to the heel of Esau, so he was named Jacob. Isaac was sixty years old when they were born."

JUDGES 13: 2-5
(Announcement of the Conception of Samson and Purpose for his Birth.)

"At that time there was a man named Manoah from the town of Zorah. He was a member of the tribe of Dan. His wife had never been able to have children. The Lord's angel appeared to her and said, You have never been able to have children, <u>but you will soon be pregnant and have a son.</u> Be sure not to drink any wine or beer, or eat any forbidden food; and after your son is born, you must never cut his hair because <u>from the day of his birth he will be dedicated to God as a Nazirite. He will begin the work of rescuing Israel from the Philistines.</u>"

I KINGS 13: 1, 2
(Announcement of Josiah's Birth c. 300 Years Before He Was Even Formed in the Womb.)

"And behold, a man of God came out of Judah by the word of the Lord to Bethel. Jeroboam was standing by the altar to burn incense. And the man cried against the altar by the word of the Lord, and said, O altar, altar, thus says the Lord: <u>Behold a son shall be born to the house of David, Josiah by name; and he shall sacrifice upon you the priests of the high places who burn incense upon you, and men's bones shall be burned upon you.</u>"

II KINGS 23: 16-18
(c. 625 B.C. Josiah Fulfills the 300 Year Old Prophecy About Him.)

"<u>And as Josiah turned, he saw the tombs there on the mount; and he sent and took the bones out of the tombs, and burned them upon the altar, and defiled it, according to the word of the Lord which the man of God proclaimed who had predicted these things.</u> Then he said, What is yonder monument that I see? And the men of the city told him<u>, It is the tomb of the man of God who came from Judah and predicted these things which you have done against the altar at Bethel.</u> And he said, Let him be; let no man move his bones. So they let his bones alone, with the bones of the prophet who came out of Samaria."

I Chronicles 22: 6-11
(Solomon's Birth and Purpose.)

"Then he [David] called for Solomon his son, and charged him to build a house for the Lord, the God of

29

Israel. David said to Solomon, My son, I had it in my heart to build a house to the name of the Lord my God. But the word of the Lord came to me saying, You have shed much blood and have waged great wars; you shall not build a house to My Name, because you have shed so much blood before Me upon the earth. <u>Behold, a son shall be born to you; he shall be a man of peace. I will give him peace from all his enemies round about; for his name shall be Solomon, (In Hebrew "Solomon" means "Peaceful.") and I will give peace and quiet to Israel in his days.</u>

<u>He shall build a house for My Name.</u> He shall be My son, and I will be his father, and I will establish his royal throne in Israel forever. Now, my son, the Lord be with you, so that you may succeed in building the house of the Lord your God, as He has spoken concerning you."

Luke 1: 11-17

(Announcement of the Conception And Purpose of John the Baptist.)

"An angel of the Lord appeared to [Zechariah], standing at the right side of the altar where the incense was burned. When Zechariah saw him, he was alarmed and felt afraid. But the angel said to him, Don't be afraid, Zechariah! God has heard your prayer, and <u>your wife Elizabeth will bear you a son. You are to name him John.</u> How glad and happy you will be, and how happy many others will be when he is born! He will be a great man in the Lord's sight. He must not drink any wine or strong drink. <u>From his</u>

very birth he will be filled with the Holy Spirit, and he will bring back many of Israel to the Lord their God. He will go ahead of the Lord, strong and mighty like the prophet Elijah. He will bring fathers and children together again; he will turn disobedient people back to the way of thinking of the righteous; he will get the Lord's people ready for Him."

Isaiah 7: 14
(Announcement of the Messiah's Birth c. 700 years before He was born.)

"Therefore the Lord Himself shall give you a sign; Behold a virgin shall conceive, and bear a son, and shall call his name Immanuel."

Isaiah 9: 6
(Announcement of the Messiah's many names c. 700 years before He Was Formed in the Womb.)

"For unto us a child is born, unto us a son is given; and the government shall be upon his shoulder: and his name shall be called Wonderful, Counselor, The mighty God, The everlasting Father, The Prince of Peace."

Luke 1: 26-33
(Announcement of the Conception and Purpose of Jesus the Christ.)

"In the sixth month the angel Gabriel was sent from God to a city of Galilee named Nazareth, to a virgin betrothed to a man whose name was Joseph, of the house of David; and the virgin's name was Mary. And he came to her and said, Hail, O favoured one, the Lord is with you! But she was greatly troubled at the saying, and considered in her mind what sort of greeting this might be. And the angel said to her, Do not be afraid, Mary, for you have found favor with God. And behold, <u>you will conceive in your womb and bear a son, and you shall call his name Jesus</u>. ("Jesus" is the Greek form of the Hebrew "Joshua" which means "Saviour.") <u>He will be great, and will be called the Son of the Most High; and the Lord God will give to him the throne of his father David, and he will reign over the house of Jacob for ever; and of His kingdom there will be no end.</u>"

Luke 2: 21

"And at the end of eight days, when he was circumcised, he was called Jesus, the name given by the angel <u>before he was conceived in the womb.</u>"

John 18: 37

"Pilate said to [Jesus], So you are a king? Jesus answered, You say that I am a king. <u>For this I was born, and for this I have come into the world, to bear witness to the truth.</u> Every one who is of the truth hears my voice."

Proverbs 16: 4

"<u>Everything the Lord has made has its destiny.</u>"

Let no one think God is haphazard just because He is prolific. Our minds sputter and short out at Divine Purpose for every child conceived within every womb.

"Before I (Isaiah) was born, the Lord chose me and appointed me to be His servant." (Isaiah 49:1)

"You will soon be pregnant and have a son…He (Samson) will begin the work of rescuing Israel from the Philistines." (Judges 13: 3-5)

"But God in His grace chose me (Paul) even before I was born, and called me to serve Him." (Galatians 1: 15)

It is very easy for this writer to know that God forms and fashions every baby in the womb. Even before I knew God, I knew a baby was a miracle. That knowledge requires no leap of faith, no mental gyrations. All one has to do is see a sonogram or a drawing of a 3 month old baby in the womb. All one has to do is see, hear, smell or feel a baby. That is miracle enough.

What is harder for the mind to grasp is that every baby God is forming in every womb will have a unique purpose here on earth. The mind boggles at Divine Purpose for every baby in the womb, at Divine Purpose for every human being on earth. But the mind shorts out only when hordes of babies world-wide are seen or envisioned. If one sees one baby, especially if that one baby is the fruit of one's own womb, the mind can indeed comprehend Divine Purpose for each baby.

It is when we scope en masse that meaning and worth and miracle become lost, incomprehensible. The Bible says God's eye is on the sparrow. (Matthew 10:29) The Bible constantly exhorts us to focus on the one, on the minute particular, on the individual. God does just that. He sees each child of His creation as though he/she were His only child. That's how God is. We always wind our way back to God's way, God's viewpoint.

"For my thoughts are not your thoughts, neither are your ways My ways, says the Lord. For as the heavens are higher than the earth, so are My ways higher than your ways and My thoughts than your thoughts." (Isaiah 55: 8,9)

Man's thoughts say, There are multiples of millions of swollen bellies world-wide. Every one of those babies can't possibly have a Divine Purpose for being.

Man's thoughts say, There are multiples of millions of fiery stars universe-wide. Every one of those stars can't possibly have a Divine Purpose for being.

Man's thoughts say, There are multiples of millions of birds earth-wide. Every one of those birds can't possibly have a Divine Purpose for being.

Man's thoughts say, I can't understand how there could be Divine Purpose for every thing and every one. I don't believe it because I can't comprehend it.

Let no man think the Creator like the creature.

"Every thing the Lord has made has its destiny." Proverbs 16:4

Let no man think the Creator limited just because His creatures are.

"For who hath known the mind of the Lord, that he may instruct Him?" I Corinthians 2:16

Who but God could make a people (the Jews) and an enduring faith (Judaeo-Christian) out of an aging Mesopotamian wandering 4,000 years ago in dusty obscurity with a post-menopausal wife? Surely no one who met this couple could have considered them that unique. But God had a Divine Purpose for Abraham and Sarah. Through the miracle of their son Isaac's birth, He would beget a people to birth His Own Son. They were decidedly "ordinary" people whom God purposed for extraordinary destinies because Abraham simply believed God. The father of our faith's sole distinction was that he knew and believed the Father of us all. That doesn't sound like such earth-shaking stuff, but it was.

And how about Abraham and Sarah's parents? Ordinary people. Yet without them, there wouldn't have been an Abraham or a Sarah. Little things. Big destinies. Little things. Little destinies. A word. An act. A prayer. A road taken. Simple, ordinary things in simple, ordinary lives can save whole cities and civilizations. One ordinary person can help or save or succor or rescue one other ordinary person. Divine Purpose.

The Lord chose Isaiah even before he was born to call Israel back to Him. In the womb God gave Isaiah the capacity for prophetic speech: "He made my words as sharp as a sword...He made me like an arrow, sharp and ready for use." (Isaiah 49:2)

Paul the Apostle's life of service to God was ordained by God even before Paul's birth in Tarsus. (Galatians 1:15)

Jeremiah, the prophet, was consecrated to God even before his conception! (Jeremiah 1:5) God purposed the birth and mission of Jeremiah before Jeremiah's parents even conceived him.

Does God have foreknowledge of babies who are going to be conceived even before they are conceived? Of course, He does. He's God.

Does God know the personalities babies in the womb will have before they are born? Does He know what that tiny baby growing in secret in your womb will be like when he or she is an adult? "Your son will live like a wild donkey; he will be against everyone, and everyone will be against him." (Genesis 16:12)

God is God. He doesn't have to mark time awaiting developments and outcomes. He is beyond time and space and matter. All the days He has allotted to each of us have been reckoned before any of them has even begun. (Psalm 139:16)

We are all created by God and we all have a Divine Purpose for being here on the earth. We are not told in the Bible all the reasons for every birth, but we are told that God purposes one thing for all people.

God's will throughout the Bible from the Genesis to the Revelation is that each child He brings into this world will realize He is Father. Only when we know our Father can the glory and purpose He meant for each of us as His children be properly unfolded and fulfilled.

Before Isaiah knew his Father, he was a man of unclean lips using the verbal talents God had bred in him for selfish ends. (Isaiah 6:5,6)

Before Paul met his Father, he ran the rocky roads of the Middle East railing against the Light. (Acts 9:1-9) After Paul encountered his Father on the road to Damascus, his Father used the desires for debate and travel He had bred in him to "turn the whole world upside down." (Acts 17:6)

Jeremiah, the weeping prophet, was one of the blessed. He not only knew his Father as a young child, but he knew his Father had conceived him for a purpose. (Jeremiah 1:1-10) In his long life of faithfulness to his Father, Jeremiah was made a laughing stock, put in dungeons and carried away to Egypt. He counted the trying circumstances of his life as nothing compared to the certainty of knowing who he was and Who had created him. "For I am called by Thy name, O Lord God of hosts." (Jeremiah 15:16)

The purpose of God for all flesh is that each may know Him regardless of our physical state or circumstances. Let no man deny the overwhelming testimony of Scripture to purpose and even glory in the midst of pain, poverty and disease!

He wants us individually to call him, "Abba, Father." (Romans 8:15) His stated, consistent desire is to love and to be loved by His children.

(John 13:1; Romans 8:35; Galatians 2:20; I John 3:16; Deuteronomy 7:8; Jeremiah 31:3)

But individually and collectively we have rejected our true Father. The post-Edenic history of man is a dramatic testimony to the love and forbearance of a Father whose children have not only denied His Paternity but have called stellar dust and terrestrial slime Abba.

Yet, yet all heaven rejoices when just one child comes Home again. (Luke 15:7)

The Father continued and continues to call down the corridors of time:

"Come unto Me all ye that are weary and are heavy laden, and I will give you rest." (Matthew 11:28)

"I am your God and will take care of you until you are old and your hair is gray. I made you and will care for you; I will give you help and rescue you." (Isaiah 46:4)

Whether you or I can comprehend the Father's ability to love, seek out, persevere with and embrace every person is immaterial. He is God the Father. No child of His slips through the cracks.

The good news to the despairing, the cynical, the confused is every thing and every one matters. There is a unique Divine Purpose for your life, for the life of the child you are carrying, for the child you have fathered. God has created that child for a purpose.

The bad news is there are enemies out there who tell seductive lies. These lies kill babies in the womb.

The first lie is: You don't have a baby in your belly. You have fetal tissue inside your womb. Fetal tissue is just bones, muscles, hair, eyes, noses, mouths, sinews, hands, hearts, brains, ovaries, kidneys, penises, toes, fingernails.

The second lie is: That fetal-tissued baby is yours. You own him or her. You can choose to kill that fetal-tissued baby or you can choose to carry him or her to term. You have a right to do whatever you want with what you own.

The third lie is: You should kill that baby because you are poor. Poor people shouldn't have babies. Poor people should kill because they are poor.

The fourth lie is: You should kill that baby because he or she is handicapped, not-perfect. Handicapped, not-perfect babies should be killed.

The fifth lie is: You should kill that baby because you are young and unmarried. Young, unmarried girls can't have babies who could ever have any kind of meaningful life.

The sixth lie is: You should kill that one baby because you already have enough babies.

The seventh lie is: You should kill your baby because a baby will interrupt your life. An uninterrupted life is worth killing for.

There are many more lies out there. The Lie breeds many lies. The Lie is very responsive to pressure and objections. New lies must constantly be hatched to put down pressures and meet objections.

The practitioners and participants in abortions are a hopeless, jaded lot who have lost all concept of the sanctity of all forms of human life, of God's existence and intervention in miserable lives and of the redemptive power of suffering.

They share with most a microscopic concentration on their own lives. They ask only those questions which relate back to their own lives: What about my life? What about my body? What about my rights? What about my career? What about my money? What about my suffering? What will this require of me? Can I handle this? I, me, my, mine.

If, by chance, they ask questions about the baby's life, the baby's welfare, the baby's suffering, the baby's rights, the Lie kicks in. What baby? It's not really a baby. You are filled with fetal tissue.

If your basic premise is a lie, all that proceeds from it is not true. The lie that reduces a baby in the womb to a medical phrase allows the murder itself because it reduces the reality and holiness of all human life to inane verbiage. The projections from that lie upon all kinds of human life become insidious and frightening.

If certain "kinds" of human life are not "real" human life and are not therefore sacred, all "kinds" of human life are up for grabs and subject to whim and regulation.

For example: Those "kinds" of people, world-wide, who are poor and who live in abject poverty don't have lives worth living because some unspecified degree of money and means makes life "worth" living. That popular lie begins to work its evil. People living worthless lives in awful situations should not be allowed to have children who will lead worthless lives, too. We who have decided this will give them contraceptives and RU486 pills and sterilization programs so they will not bring any more poor people into the world. If they don't submit to these measures out of some misguided, primitive desire for procreation, we will build abortion clinics for them. If we can't educate them not to have children, we'll provide killing fields so they won't re-produce themselves. Or we will regulate and penalize them financially if they don't want to kill their babies. We'll devise better and better measures to discriminate against and stamp out poor people.

The Bible does not share the world's current view of the poor and their babies. The Father has always reached out to His children who are materially and/or spiritually poor.

"But I am poor and needy; yet the Lord thinketh upon me." (Psalm 40:17)

The Bible says God "raiseth up the poor out of the dust, and lifteth up the beggar from the dunghill, to set them among princes, and to make them inherit the throne of glory." (I Samuel 2:8)

Who of us would presume to judge which baby from whose poverty-stricken womb may be destined for princedom or heavenly thrones? Search out the leaders of our world and tell me that none of them came from poverty or from unfortunate circumstances. And tell me that all those who will be honored in the Kingdom will only come from advantaged parents.

"I will also leave in the midst of thee an afflicted and poor people, and they shall trust in the name of the Lord." (Zephaniah 3:12)

Have we lost the reality, the Truth that a poor and afflicted person who trusts in God is of as much worth as a rich and healthy person?

"There are those who rebel against the light, who are not acquainted with its ways, and do not stay in its paths. The murderer rises in the dark, that he may kill the poor and needy; and in the night is a thief."(Job 24: 13, 14)

To murder babies just because it is assumed they will inherit poverty is spiritual blindness and sin. Because a baby will be poor and needy when he or she is born, does not mean he or she will be of no value.

"I have also seen this example of wisdom under the sun, and it seemed great to me. There was a little city with few men in it; and a great king came against it and besieged it, building great siegeworks against it. But there was found in it a poor wise man, and he by his wisdom delivered the city. Yet no one remembered that poor man. But I say that wisdom is better than might, though the poor man's wisdom is despised, and his words are not heeded." (Ecclesiastes 9:13-16)

One poor, wise man delivered a whole city from destruction. How many poor, wise, various-colored baby boys and girls who would have been capable of redeeming our inner cities have we torn out of their mothers' wombs in the busy, strategically-planned abortion clinics planted in the bowels of our cities?

Map out most of the killing fields and you will find they are located near the poor.

Poor people, Awaken! You are targeted by this army of death.

Jesus was "anointed to preach the gospel to the poor." (Luke 4:18)

When He walked the earth, "the poor (had) the gospel preached to them." (Matthew 11:5)

In the Sermon on the Plain He cried, "Blessed are ye poor: for yours is the kingdom of God. Blessed are ye that hunger now: for ye shall be filled. Blessed are ye that weep now: for ye shall laugh." (Luke 6:20, 21) He preached and lived an ethic opposed to the modern view of the poor. Jesus even hallowed need.

To buy the lie that the poor don't live worthy human lives reduces them to a sub-human mass that targets them for attempted extinction one way or another. So far, we only try to control the numbers of the poor by encouraging, counseling and facilitating the deaths of their babies. So far.

Whenever poverty is viewed as sub-human existence rather than valid human life and even possibility for sanctity, that particular "kind" of human life is up for grabs.

It must be observed in passing that this lie is embroidered with a gaudy, see-through pastiche of facile humanism: Poor, poor people. Daddy will help you. Daddy knows best. You're not able to discern what is best for you. You're only allowed to have one baby or no baby. We'll help you kill all the others you conceive. Here's a nice, big piece of bread. Why are you still crying?

Babies for bread.

Because America is a nation founded under God whose laws and morality were meant to reflect the Bible, she has always been on the forefront of need. Her doors have been thrown open to the poor, the needy, the afflicted. Her purses have emptied incalculable amounts of money upon the poor and devastated of this planet. Great numbers of our people have devoted their lives to the poor and afflicted on every continent. There has never been a nation who has so faithfully lived the Judaeo-Christian ethic toward the poor.

We must realize, however, that those values and our obedience to them were Bible-based values. America has been putting into practice commands and exhortations found in God's Word. We did not get together and organically hatch these ideas and deeds of mercy out of thin air. We were guided by the injunctions of Scripture. Biblical principles pervaded our land and shaped our responses. We were not perfectly obedient, perfectly behaved, but we have acted.

The poor have always been a priority with the Father. America once believed helping the poor meant food, shelter, clothing, spiritual food and tending. She has never until recently believed helping the poor meant killing their babies.

As soon as God gave the wandering Jews a land, He began making provisions for His poor children. He told the Jews to till the land for six years, but "the seventh year thou shalt let it rest and lie still; that the poor of thy people may eat." (Exodus 23:11) From the beginning of Scripture God has enjoined us to provide for the needs of the poor out of our abundance however great or small.

Jesus said, "When thou makest a dinner or supper, call not thy friends, nor thy brethren, neither thy kinsman, nor thy rich neighbors...But when thou makest a feast, call the poor, the maimed, the lame, the blind." (Luke 14:12, 13) And in response to God's Word America has always reached out to feed, clothe and tend the poor and handicapped.

It is to our eternal shame that we now kill them in the womb.

"Blessed is he that considereth the poor: The Lord will deliver him in time of trouble." (Psalm 41:1)

"They would that we should remember the poor." (Galatians 2:10)

The poor, the needy, the suffering are at the heart of God's Word. He counsels us to go to them, feed them, preach the Good News to them, set up hostels and sanctuaries for them. He does not counsel us to drag their babies from their wombs so they will be population-controlled.

Nor does He counsel or sanction us to kill the lame, the blind, the handicapped babies in the womb.

When I was pregnant with my third child, the doctor suggested I have amniocentesis. I soon learned that this is another medical word which hides a killer. One of the results of this procedure will give the parents prior-to-birth knowledge of a handicapped child. If the test shows that the baby is handicapped, many doctors will offer the distressed mother the option of killing the child. Many mothers exercise that option. Many of us have refused the test and have told our doctors that we would love, care for and raise a handicapped child or a "normal" child.

Surely anyone who has reflected on this life at all must know that there are conditions of the soul and mind more distressing, harder to bear and more disturbing than a handicapped baby. Most of us who have lived long enough have witnessed blessings, miracles, inspirations and "angels unaware" (Hebrews 13:2) through handicapped children.

In the Gospels, Christ's hands of compassion are forever on the lame, the blind, the dumb, the leprous, the insane, the epileptic, the palsied, the feeble-minded, the deaf. He sought them out. He encouraged them to seek Him.

One of the most powerful sentences in the New Testament was spoken by a man handicapped by blindness from birth. Jesus had given him sight. The healing became a theological football between the healed one, his parents and a type of church people called Pharisees. The Pharisees wanted the man to admit that Jesus was a sinner rather than the Messiah.

These disputes were too much for the uneducated, newly-sighted man. In frustration he cried out to the Pharisees, "Whether He be a sinner or no, I know not; one thing I know, that, whereas I was blind, now I see." (John 9:25)

One of the wisest affirmations which has echoed throughout our history came from the lips of a man handicapped from birth.

These are valuable points, but they are all subordinate to the main point: A baby physically handicapped from the womb is of as much worth as a baby not physically handicapped from the womb.

The lies which condemn poor babies to death are busy condemning handicapped babies to death.

Handicapped babies have become relegated to the same sub-human status as poor babies. This child is handicapped. He or she will never live a really meaning-full life. A meaningful life must be a healthy life.

Babies in the womb are killed for lack of money. Babies in the womb are killed for lack of health. The values begin to emerge—money and health.

WEALTH AND HEALTH = VALUABLE LIFE
POVERTY AND SICKNESS = WORTHLESS LIFE

Does America really believe these equations?
We kill as though we do.
Have we been deceived?

When the killing of babies God is fashioning in the womb starts, there is no end to the reasons for killing. If a poor and a handicapped baby can be sucked out and disposed of, what other "kinds" of babies can be dispatched?

How about healthy girl babies? Selective abortions. World-wide millions and millions of babies are aborted just because they happen to be female instead of male.

How about perfectly healthy babies of both sexes who would not be poor?

We kill those kinds of babies, too—every minute.

Some of you must be thinking, My God, that's insane! What have we got against babies?

One of the main things we have against babies is that they alter our lives.

If you are young and/or unmarried, a baby will alter your life. If you have four children, another baby will alter your life. If you have a career, a baby will alter your life.

We kill babies all the time just because they will alter our lives. We only want our lives to be changed when we want to change our lives.

We may mask these kinds of murders with a different rhetoric, but the truth remains:

I was not married. I killed the baby in my womb because I didn't want to raise a baby alone, etc. I didn't want my life to be altered in that way at that time.

I already had two children. I killed the third child in my womb because I didn't feel like having another child. I didn't want the status quo of my family to be changed.

I was working hard at my career. I killed my baby because I didn't want to quit work, get babysitters, etc. I didn't want my career path altered at that time in that way.

We kill babies in the womb who are healthy, who will not be raised in poverty just because we don't feel like having them.

As can be seen, once human beings of any classification (poor, handicapped) are labeled "not fit," all classifications are up for random, whimsical, wholesale slaughter. Today we are killing all "kinds" of human babies in the womb: poor babies, rich babies, 2" babies, 20" babies, sick babies, well babies, black, white, red, brown and yellow babies.

When one tiny category of human life becomes fair game, it is open season on all categories. When just one human life is considered not sacred, not holy, all humans are profaned and threatened.

She's old. Let her die. He's sick. Let him die. "Euthanasia," "Right to Die" are other words which mask a murderer.

Or let's kill them before they are really dead so we can harvest their kidneys and hearts. Or she has a right to die, to kill herself. I love her. I'll help her. Perversion after perversion. Abomination upon abomination. Pray God none who read this ever becomes sick or old or despondent!

Because if womb life is disposable now, all of us become disposable sooner or later.

When certain kinds of human beings can be bagged and sold by the pound, every human being is on the chopping block.

A society which has the SANCTION to kill any kind of human life has the POTENTIAL to kill all kinds of human life.

When we began to kill babies in the womb and justified that act, we began to kill old and sick people and justified that. When we began to kill babies in the womb and justified that act, we began to aid and abet suicide and justified that.

The evil is spreading. No category of human life should feel safe from this army of death.

What ideal human being are we trying to form and fashion in our madness?

Not long ago a short, dark-haired, dark-eyed Prussian tried to form and fashion a race of tall, blond-haired, blue-eyed humans. Is the sick, pitiful, aging monster within us trying to form and fashion a race of humans who are healthy, wealthy, ageless and immune from all diseases and problems?

Who is targeted next as we kill our way to human perfection?

The Bible is clear and unequivocal. The baby in the womb is God's creation. He Alone is the Author of life and Lord of death.

"In His hand is the life of every living thing and the breath of all mankind." Job 12:10

He has a unique purpose for each human being who is conceived in a womb. Every one has a distinctive, if not readily discernible, reason for being here on the planet. The poor, the handicapped, the healthy, male and female babies were all allowed to be conceived by Him for reasons of blessings, lessons, words, growths, compassions, salvations, redemptions, missions, fatherhoods, motherhoods, earthly offices and heavenly thrones. (I Samuel 2:8)

We proceed from Him and we shall stand before Him on the Day of Judgment. The very breath we draw is at His discretion. Those who destroy human life in the womb should know they have made themselves enemy to the God Who fashioned them in the womb for a purpose and gave them life.

We have sown the wind.
What harvest whirls ahead?

JUDGMENT

IN THE UNITED STATES AN UNWANTED OR HANDICAPPED BABY IS ABORTED EVERY 21 SECONDS. WHAT DOES THE BIBLE HAVE TO SAY ABOUT THAT?

Jeremiah 2: 32, 34

"...yet my people have forgotten Me days without number...<u>Also in thy skirts is found the blood of the souls of the poor innocents.</u>"

Isaiah 49: 15

"<u>Can a woman forget her sucking child, that she should not have compassion on the son of her womb? yea, they may forget, yet will I not forget thee.</u>"

Psalm 27: 10

"<u>When my father and my mother forsake me, then the Lord will take me up.</u>"

Lamentations 4: 3, 4

"Even a mother wolf will nurse her cubs, <u>but my people are like ostriches, cruel to their young. They let their babies die of hunger and thirst.</u>"

Amos 1: 13

"The people of Ammon (and America) have sinned again and again, and for this I will certainly punish them. In their wars for more territory they even ripped open pregnant women."

Psalm 22: 9-11

"But Thou art He that took me out of the womb: Thou didst make me hope when I was upon my mother's breasts. I was cast upon Thee from the womb: Thou art my God from my mother's belly. Be not far from me; for trouble is near; for there is none to help."

Proverbs 24: 11, 12

"Rescue those being led away to death; hold back those staggering toward slaughter. If you say, 'But we knew nothing about this,' does not He Who weighs the heart perceive it? Does not He Who guards your life know it? Will not He repay each person according to what he has done?"

Jeremiah 4: 22, 31

"For my people is foolish, they have not known Me; they are sottish children, and they have none understanding: they are wise to do evil, but to do good they have no knowledge...I heard a voice as of a woman in travail, and the anguish as of her that bringeth forth her first child, the voice of the daughter of Zion, that bewaileth herself, <u>that spreadeth her hands, saying, Woe is me now! for my soul is wearied because of murderers.</u>"

Proverbs 6: 17

"There are six things the Lord hates, seven that are detestable to Him: haughty eyes, a lying tongue, <u>hands that shed innocent blood…</u>"

Ezekiel 16: 1-22

"The Lord spoke to me again. Mortal man, He said, point out to Jerusalem (America) what disgusting things she has done. Tell (America) what the Sovereign Lord is saying to her:

…When you were born, no one cut your umbilical cord or washed you or rubbed you with salt or wrapped you in cloths. No one took enough pity on you to do any of these things for you. When you were born, no one loved you. You were thrown out in an open field. Then I passed by and saw you squirming in your own blood. You were covered with blood, but I wouldn't let you die. I made you grow like a healthy plant. You grew strong and tall and became a young woman. Your breasts were well-formed, and your hair had grown, but you were naked. As I passed by again, I saw that the time had come for you to fall in love. I covered your naked body with my coat and promised to love you. Yes, I made a marriage covenant with you, and you became mine.

This is what the Sovereign Lord says:

Then I took water and washed the blood off you. I rubbed olive oil on your skin. I dressed you in embroidered gowns and gave you shoes of the best leather, a linen headband, and a silk cloak. I put jewels on you—bracelets and necklaces. I gave you a nose ring and earrings and a beautiful crown to wear. You had ornaments of gold and silver, and you always wore clothes of embroidered linen and silk. You ate bread made from the best flour, and had honey and olive oil to eat. Your beauty was dazzling and you became a queen. You became famous in every nation for your perfect beauty, because I was the one who made you so lovely.

This is what the Sovereign Lord says.

But you took advantage of your beauty and fame to sleep with everyone who came along. You used some of your clothes to decorate your places of worship, and just like a prostitute, you gave yourself to everyone. You took the silver and gold jewelry that I had given you, used it to make male images, and committed adultery with them. You took the embroidered clothes I gave you and put them on the images, and you offered to the images the olive oil and incense I had given you. I gave you food—the best flour, olive oil and honey—but you offered it as a sacrifice to win the favor of idols.

This is what the Sovereign Lord says (to America).

Then you took the sons and daughters you had borne Me and offered them as sacrifices to idols. Wasn't it bad enough to be unfaithful to Me, without taking My children and sacrificing them to idols? During your disgusting life as a prostitute you never once remembered your childhood—when you were naked, squirming in your own blood."

Jeremiah 9: 1-3, 20, 21

"O that my head were waters, and my eyes a fountain of tears, that I might weep day and night for the slain of the daughter of my people!
O that I had in the desert a wayfarers' lodging place, that I might leave my people and go away from them! For they are all adulterers, a company of treacherous men. They bend their tongue like a bow; falsehood and not truth has grown strong in the land; for they proceed from evil to evil, and they do not know me, says the Lord...Hear, O women, the word of the Lord, and let your ear receive the word of His mouth; teach to your daughters a lament, and each to her neighbor a dirge. For death has come up into our windows, it has entered our palaces, cutting off the children from the streets."

Matthew 18: 1-7, 10

"At that time the disciples came to Jesus, saying, Who is the greatest in the kingdom of heaven? And calling to Him a child, He put him in the midst of them and said, Truly, I say to you, unless you turn and become like children, you will never enter the kingdom of heaven. Whoever humbles himself like this child, he is the greatest in the kingdom of heaven. Whoever receives one such child in My Name receives Me; but whoever causes one of these little ones who believe in Me to sin, it would be better for him to have a great millstone fastened round his neck and to be drowned in the depth of the sea. Woe to the world for temptations to sin!

For it is necessary that temptations come, but woe to the man by whom the temptation comes…See that you do not despise one of these little ones; for I tell you that in heaven their angels always behold the face of My Father Who is in heaven."

Psalm 102: 18-20

"Let this be recorded for a generation to come, so that a people yet unborn may praise the Lord: that He looked down from His holy height, from heaven the Lord looked at the earth, to hear the groans of the prisoners, to set free those who were doomed to die."

"The Lord spoke to me. Mortal man, He said, tell your people what happens when I bring war to a land. The people of that country choose one of their number to be a watchman. When he sees the enemy approaching, he sounds the alarm to warn everyone. If someone hears it but pays no attention and the enemy comes and kills him, then he is to blame for his own death. His death is his own fault, because he paid no attention to the warning. If he had paid attention, he could have escaped. If, however, the watchman sees the enemy coming and does not sound the alarm, the enemy will come and kill those sinners, but I will hold the watchman responsible for their death.

Now, mortal man, I am making you a watchman for the nation...You must pass on to them the warnings I give you. If I announce that an evil man is going to die but you do not warn him to change his ways so that he can save his life, then he will die, still a sinner, and I will hold you responsible for his death. If you do warn an evil man and he doesn't stop sinning, he will die, still a sinner, but your life will be spared." Ezekiel 33:1-9

It is crystal clear in the Scriptures that Bible-believing Jews and Christians are to warn people of impending danger. If we know the enemy is upon them and we fail to warn them, we are held responsible.

We are our brother's keeper. (Genesis 4:9) We are involved, engaged people. We who know God and believe His Word are to sound the alarm loud and clear when a person or a society is in danger of reaping the whirlwind.

"Upon your walls, O Jerusalem (America), I have set watchmen; all the day and all the night they shall never be silent." Isaiah 62:6

A person or a society is in danger when God's laws are abrogated. A society which practices and/or puts into law something contrary to the express laws of God and the repeated teachings of the Testaments has put itself in opposition to God and is in peril of judgment.

Because of the universal practice and legal sanctions of abortion, our culture is on a collision course with God Almighty.

The Bible consistently teaches that God causes life to begin and to develop in the womb. That baby in the womb is God the Father's—not our own. If we kill a baby in the womb, we are killing some one God has brought into existence for a purpose.

The blood of that murder is upon the hands of all those who actively or passively participated in the murder. We must warn our people not to commit this abomination.

If not one sparrow dies without God's notice, can one baby squirming in its own blood escape His gaze? The Bible teaches we are more than sparrows (Matthew 10:29) and a little lower than angels (Hebrews 2:7).

The foe of those For Abortion is God. We must tell them this. The people who believe in killing babies in the womb may be deceived into thinking their opposition is just a rag-taggle, strident band of bigoted factions. That is not the truth. Their enemy is God the Creator Who opposes and eventually vanquishes those who stray from His commandments and boogie with His creations.

"Thou dost rebuke the insolent, accursed ones, who wander from Thy commandments." Psalm 119:21

The God of the Bible is not wishy-washy. He does not encourage us to be wishy-washy people.

"I know what you have done; I know that you are neither cold nor hot. How I wish you were either one or the other! But because you are lukewarm, neither hot nor cold, I am going to spit you out of My mouth!" Revelation 3:15, 16

"No servant can be the slave of two masters; he will hate one and love the other; he will be loyal to one and despise the other. You cannot serve God and money." Luke 16:13

"Jesus said to him, Anyone who starts to plow and then keeps looking back is of no use for the Kingdom of God." Luke 9:62

"You cannot drink from the Lord's cup and also from the cup of demons; you cannot eat at the Lord's table and also at the table of demons" I Corinthians 10:21

"So they worshiped the Lord, but they also worshiped their own gods." II Kings 17:33

"A person like that, unable to make up his mind and undecided in all he does, must not think he will receive anything from the Lord." James 1:7, 8

The Bible doesn't give the believer any leeway. You are either in or you are out. If you are half in and half out, you risk all the things contained in the above verses. It's the Joshua Syndrome: you either serve the Lord or you wander the wilderness unarmed.

You are either For Abortion or Against Abortion. There is no middle ground!

Rarely in the history of mankind have we had state-sponsored, medically-approved, legislated, organized, systematic, moment by moment inexorable killing of babies in the womb. Such a practice is so foreign to history, so abominable and repugnant to sane humans and so utterly opposed to God's laws that no person who is in any way associated with God and the Bible dares refrain from taking a stand Against Abortion.

But the latter half of the twentieth century is not the first time in history where there has been a period of state-sponsored infanticide.

Exodus 1:8-22 says:

"Now there arose a new king over Egypt, who did not know Joseph. And he said to his people, Behold the people of Israel are too many and too mighty for us. Come, let us deal shrewdly with them, lest they multiply, and, if war befall us, they join our enemies and fight against us and escape from the land. Therefore they set taskmasters over them to afflict them with heavy burdens; and they built for Pharaoh store-cities, Pithom and Raamses. But the more they were oppressed, the more they multiplied and the more they spread abroad. And the Egyptians were in dread of the people of Israel. So they made the people of Israel serve with rigor, and made their lives bitter with hard service, in mortar and brick, and in all kinds of work in the field; in all their work they made them serve with rigor.

Then the king of Egypt said to the Hebrew midwives, one of whom was named Shiphrah and the other Puah, When you serve as midwife to the Hebrew women, and see them upon the birthstool, if it is a son, you shall kill him; but if it is a daughter, she shall live. But the midwives feared God, and did not do as the king of Egypt commanded them but let the male children live. So the king of Egypt called the midwives, and said to them,

Why have you done this, and let the male children live? The midwives said to Pharaoh, Because the Hebrew women are not like the Egyptian women; for they are vigorous and are delivered before the midwife comes to them.

So God dealt well with the midwives; and the people multiplied and grew very strong. And because the midwives feared God He gave them families. Then Pharaoh commanded all his people. Every son that is born to the Hebrews you shall cast into the Nile, but you shall let every daughter live."

Here the state was a monarchy under pharaoh. The Jews were and had been slaves in Egypt for about 400 years. In his human wisdom pharaoh thought it would be prudent to control the population of these slaves so they wouldn't become strong enough to side with an enemy in case of war. If the enemy won, pharaoh would not only lose his slave labor but his kingdom as well.

His first strategy for "population control" was to work them so hard that some of the men would die and the rest would be too tired to have sex. But the harder they worked the Jews, the more the Jews multiplied. No matter how many cities they had the Jews build, no matter how many hours they had them work, no matter how much they beat and battered them, the Jews just kept having more and more children.

His second strategy for population control was infanticide. Pharaoh was a forward-looking ruler who felt he had the future welfare of his kingdom at stake. The ancient Egyptians, unlike their surrounding neighbors, were not known for human sacrifice, for ritual murders of children or for barbarous disregard of human life. On the contrary, they, like we, spent much time and ingenuity on the treatment of human diseases and the saving of human life. They were what we would call "civilized."

But pharaoh and his people had a problem. There were too many of a certain "kind" of people living in his land. The goal of this second strategy was limited ZPG, Zero Population Growth.

Infanticide would solve his problem. If you kill certain babies before they are born or at the moment of birth, you will certainly be able to control how many people live in a certain place at a certain time. Pharaoh felt that he was being a responsible ruler. After all, the Jewish slaves were his property to do with as he saw fit. He owned them. At that time slaves were in the same category as cattle and houses and fields and jewelry. We at the beginning of the 21st century know pharaoh was wrong. A slave is a human being just like pharaoh was. We know we don't "own" any one, intra or extra-uterine.

Once pharaoh and his cabinet were committed to infanticide as the answer to their socio-political problem, they went to the medical establishment for help. Birth has always been helped along and encouraged by the medical establishment of a culture no matter how advanced the state of that science.

The easiest way to kill children is to kill them either before they are born or right after they are born. They are totally defenseless at those times and have not had enough time to foster the emotional attachments which make killing them so much more delicate. Midwives have been and still are in some places an integral part of the birth process. Pharaoh summoned two representatives of the Jewish midwives named Shiphrah and Puah.

At that time and still in some parts of the world, women gave birth on birthing stools. Pharaoh ordered Shiphrah and Puah to have the midwives kill the Jewish boy babies as they came out of the womb, but to let the girl babies live. This was selective abortion and it was pragmatic. Male babies grew into men who could fight. The reason for the wholesale slaughter in the first place was to make sure there wouldn't be a fighting force of slaves to side with invaders.

This was many centuries before medical ethic boards or oaths, but the Jewish midwives "feared God and did not do as the king of Egypt commanded them, but let the male children live." (Ex.1:17) Obviously the Egyptian government had a task force which was appointed to oversee the slaughter. They reported back to pharaoh that his orders were not being obeyed. Pharaoh called the God-fearing medical women to give account of themselves.

The midwives lied to the government. They said that the Jewish women gave birth more quickly than Egyptian women did. They said that by the time the midwives arrived, the babies were already born and swaddled. They lied to their rulers and saved human lives because they feared the wrath of God more than the threat of man.

"So God dealt well with the midwives; and the people multiplied and grew very strong. And because the midwives feared God He gave them families." (Exodus1: 20, 21) The medical people who refused to comply with state-sponsored infanticide were blessed by the Lord of Life with families! To have children, to be a part of a loving family was the highest reward God could conceive for those faithful women.

Pharaoh's third strategy was a variation on his second strategy. If the government couldn't carry out its pragmatic plan with the collaboration of the Jewish medical establishment, if they couldn't get the Jews to kill their own, they would carry it out systematically home by home, family by family. All the people were commanded to throw every son born to a Jewish family into the Nile River.

It is likely that some baby boys survived this edict. The slave population was in the millions. (Exodus 12:37, 38) It would be impossible for the government to monitor closely every single household. But it is indisputable that countless numbers of infant boys were thrown into the Nile by their intimidated parents or by government authorities. (Acts 7:19)

The weeping, crying, gnashing of teeth in the Jewish land of Goshen must have been heard as far away as Memphis as families killed or saw killed the precious fruits of their wombs. Their grief was equaled 80 years later by the Plague of the First-Born when the Angel of Death passed over the land of Egypt and killed all the first-born children of Egypt from the first-born of pharaoh who sat on his throne to the first-born of the prisoner in the dungeon. There was such a cry throughout all of Egypt never heard before or since. (Exodus 11:6)

God may not work in our time frame, but He hears the silent cries of our aborted infants as surely as He heard the cries of the baby boys drowning in the Nile thousands of years ago. It took 80 years for the cries of the Hebrew innocents to be avenged—only 80 years for the entire land of Egypt to reap what it had sown.

And there was irony as well as justice there. God used a boy baby who had been rescued from the scheme of infanticide, Moses, to pronounce the

Plague of the First-Born on Egypt and to lead the entire slave population to freedom.

Moses, "drawn from water," saved from an aborted life, son of poverty-stricken slaves, leader of millions, servant of the Most High, to whom God gave the Commandments upon which our civilization rests, pharaoh wanted you dead.

The battle to save the lives of all babies targeted in the womb must be fought. 1,500,000 babies are killed every year just in America. This is not a fight brewing. This is a battle raging.

Hundreds of thousands of doctors, nurses, paramedicals have killed babies. Millions of American mothers have had their children murdered. Millions of American fathers have paid to have their babies disposed of. Millions of relatives and friends have given counsel or kept silent as the murders were performed. Multiples of millions in America have the blood of the poor innocents on their hands and the blood won't come off. Multiples of millions of American people are in a mobilized army dedicated to tearing babies out of the womb.

This army of death moves steadily, methodically through the corridors of America. One by one the women of America lie down, spread their legs and let vacuums or hooks or solutions or surgical instruments deliver them of dead, dismembered babies. One by one, day by day the medical establishment of America scrubs up and then goes in and kills another baby.

We have taken the sons and daughters God has given us and sacrificed them to idols. (Ezekiel 16:20,21)

We have sacrificed the children of the poor on the Altar of Money.

We have sacrificed handicapped children on the Altar of Health.

We have sacrificed millions of not-poor, not-handicapped children on the Altar of Convenience.

Our nation has abandoned the God who birthed, swaddled and tended us.

"Wasn't it bad enough to be unfaithful to Me," says the Father "without taking My children and sacrificing them to idols?"

Woe, Woe, America!

Your experts "see a cloud rising in the west (and) say at once, A shower is coming; and so it happens…(they) see the south wind blowing and say, There will be scorching heat; and it happens. You hypocrites! You know how to interpret the appearance of the earth and sky; but why do you not know how to interpret the present time? And why do you not judge for yourselves what is right?" (Luke 12:54-56)

Why, America, are you wise to discern the weather but blinded and hardened to the dark clouds and evil winds of this age?

What satanic opiate allows you not only to abort your babies but to let your aborted babies be used in experiments and to be processed for their spare parts?

When God as Creator of human life is denied, man becomes the insane monster-maker. In the middle of the twentieth century Nazi doctors implanted animal sperm in Jewish wombs just to see what would happen.

One would hope we now consider those "scientific experimenters" evil and insane. Do we?

If man is creator and womb life is cheap, may not our American scientists and medical people be trying the same things in laboratories? Interpreting the "present time," may not our experts be trying to see if animal wombs can carry human babies or if "genetically-engineered" (another medical phrase which hides a killer) identical babies can be cloned from one cell? Are our American doctors and scientists trying to see if "we" can "make" all "kinds" and "forms" of human life from the warp and woof of human cell life? May not we be evil and insane, too?

Just because the apparatus does not involve camps and ovens does not mean the same evil genius is not steadily at work in labs and facilities. Because the wolf dons the skin of the sheep does not mean he is not wolf.

All of us who worship God have repeatedly thanked the Creator for those men and women of science and medicine, believers or non-believers, who have been used by Him in life-saving and healing ministries and research. These words are not intended for those decent people.

But we must be warned that advanced technology does not equal advanced morality. Medical and scientific discoveries do not equate to moral and spiritual plateaus. An equation exists only when the individual scientist, doctor, technocrat bows to an Authority greater than his and submits his talents to that service. If he serves only himself or other men, he becomes self-serving, man-pleasing. Such a one beginning and ending with man begins ever so marginally, ever so well-intentionedly to veer off course.

When the line of inquiry into creation does not begin and end with the Creator, it wiggles farther and farther into the outer reaches of darkness. What unspeakable abominations are we committing dancing in the dark deluded by the false authorities of scientific and medical benefits and inquiry?

We who stand on the authority of Scripture must not allow ourselves to be silenced or our criticisms to be nullified by the spurious doctrine that the end justifies the means. We must not allow experiments which yield an occasional "benefit" to rest on the bodies of murdered babies. We must not yield to the lampshade-made-of-human-skin mentality. Because the light becomes less harsh does not obscure the glare of a murdered human being. Because a "benefit" may ensue does not cover the evil of a baby murdered for its parts.

All Bible-believing Christians and Jews know that "a corrupt tree brings forth evil fruit...neither can a corrupt tree bring forth good fruit." (Matthew 7:17, 18) We know the end is irrevocably wedded to and child of the means.

One cannot kill one's way to the good!

"You have plowed wickedness, you have reaped iniquity." Hosea 10:13

"Be not deceived; God is not mocked: for whatsoever a man soweth, that shall he also reap." Galatians 6:7

The laws of seed and harvest observed in nature parable laws planted in us by the Creator. God is not mocked. If we sow death and destruction, we will reap death and destruction. The Bible and all of nature counsel us to stay within the Law.

"There is a way which seems right to a man, but its end is the way of death." Proverbs 14:12

To those outside the sanity and authority of the Bible, it may seem right to kill a baby in the womb in order to use his or her organs and cells for research and experimentation.
The End is Research and Experiment.
The Means is Baby Death.

If the killing of a baby is the foundation, if the baby's organs and/or cells are the structure, the name of that house is the House of Death.
The perversion which can kill a baby in the womb or in a petri dish in the name of and for the sake of scientific or medical advance will only yield our society the fruits of destruction.
THAT WHICH RESTS UPON A MURDER RECLINES IN BLOOD.
We must not be deceived about means and ends. Death-dealers are never life-bringers.

The Bible admonishes us to warn our people when we see an enemy approaching. Because Godly men and women were not vigilant, the enemy is already within our walls. The fight is now person to person, household to household, street by street, town by town, law by law, Word by word to drive the enemy of abortion from our nation.

Only God will judge this writer and all others who knew abortion was an abomination and did not warn loud enough, did not fight long enough and hard enough to repel the evil invader. May God forgive our silent complicity and our assumption of a fighting force which was not there.

At His birth our Lord knew what it was like to be an infant and "have trouble near; for there is none to help." (Psalm 22:11) He Who was born to save men from the bitter harvest of sin was targeted by the state for death under Herod the Great. Herod "killed all the male children in Bethlehem and in all the region who were two years old and under" (Matthew 2:16) hoping to catch the Messiah in his broad net of infanticide.

The Word chose to become flesh and live among us in and under some of the very conditions now targeted for population control.

Our Lord chose to be conceived in a very young girl who was not yet married. Matthew 1:18

He chose to be born bereft in a barn. Luke 2:7

He chose to live in a town whose very name means "Despised." Matthew 2:23

He chose to be part of the homeless population. Luke 9:"58

He chose to associate with and to call into service those considered the scum of society. Luke 5:30; Mark 2:15, 16

The state hounded such a One who lived such a life from the cradle to the cross.

What did this Jesus, Whom the state wanted dead as a child, have to say about the holiness and value of children?

"Truly, I say to you, unless you turn and become like children, you will never enter the kingdom of heaven. Whoever humbles himself like this child, he is the greatest in the kingdom of heaven." Matthew 18:3, 4

Here Jesus makes a child the incarnate symbol of the best of heaven. Instead of considering them not fully human because of their youth, He advises us that babes and children are the prized, visible parables of the state of heaven itself and of the spirit of all those who will inherit eternal life.

In casual casuistry you may say, But a child is not a baby in the womb. You are mixing apples and oranges.

Is a small orange less an orange?

Is a tiny little apple not an apple?

A baby is a baby is a baby.

Jesus said of John the Baptist, the surprise post-menopausal child of Elizabeth and Zacharias, "Truly I say to you, among those born of women there has arisen no one greater than John the Baptist." (Matthew 11:11)

It was this same c. 12"-14" John, only six months old in his mother's womb, "who leaped for joy" in Elizabeth's belly when Mary came to tell about her own pregnancy. (Luke 1:44)

The Baptist growing in secret in his mother's womb knew the Lordship of Him Who was just conceived in Mary's womb. (Luke 1:39-44) Do our children have feelings and emotions when they are still in the womb? If a child is being dissected arm by leg by head in our womb, is that child "feeling" pain? John the Baptist understood, felt some type of joy, exhilaration. Surely our womb children feel and cry out in agony during dismemberment. All the silent screams!

The Bible is filled with people whom God called when they were still in the womb or before they were even conceived. (Isaiah 49:1,2,5; Jeremiah 1:4,5; Galatians 1:15; Genesis 16:7-12) The Bible claims not only awareness in the womb and sanctity for womb life, but purpose for every child conceived.

He Who had been saved from infant death hallowed the infant child as living embodiment of God's kingdom.

"See that you do not despise one of these little ones," says the Lord, "for I tell you that in heaven their angels always behold the face of the Father Who is in heaven." Matthew 18:10

How long, America, will we be able to kill 2", 12", 20" little ones before we incur the wrath of their avenging angels?

Some of the people in the Bible were among the "kinds" of people now allowed to be killed in the womb.

Jesus the Redeemer and Moses the Deliverer were born at times when the law of the land temporarily sanctioned infanticide. The One escaped by a flight to Egypt. The other escaped by Egyptian adoption.

Esther who saved an entire nation in exile from annihilation was an orphan. She didn't have a mother or a father.

Isaac was conceived by a woman past menopause.

John the Baptist was conceived by a woman past menopause.

Judah through whom the Messianic line comes was a child unwanted by his father.

The child who began the Moabite nation was a child of incest as was the child who was the father of the Ammonites.

Joseph of the multi-colored coat was the 11th child in a family. He was also sold into slavery and abandoned by his brothers.

Ishmael who birthed the Arab nation was an abused child cast out of his father's household.

Pharez, direct antecedent in the Messiah's blood line, was born to a woman who was unmarried and pretended to be a whore in order to conceive him.

Boaz, David's great-grandfather, was the son of a whore.

Daniel of the lion's den was separated from his parents when he was a child.

Amos came from a dirt poor shepherd's family.

Poverty, abandonment, incest, whoredom, treachery, abuse, inconvenience, unwantedness, embarrassment. The beauty of the Bible is that it pulls no punches where its heroes and heroines are involved. It is dedicated to Truth. And the truth is that in spite of the tragic, often very sinful circumstances of their births, these people were allowed to be born, to live and to impact history.

Some of these people were great heroes of our faith.

Others lived wasted lives.

But who among us is wise enough to determine ahead of time which child will live an heroic life, a wasted life or just a plain ordinary life?

And certainly a person who lives an heroic life has no more worth before God Who is no respecter of persons than one who wastes his life. (Ephesians 6:9; Romans 2:11; Colossians 3:25)

Certainly we are all sinners and all lives not consecrated to the Father are in a real and eternal sense wasted. There are no sinless births or circumstances of birth. All are born into the sinful state of man. All human beings will sooner or later mess up.

God has given us the marriage bed and the family for maximum stability and possibility in this fallen world. A child not conceived under these maximum circumstances should not be penalized to death for the behavior of his or her father and mother. It is not sane to kill a child because his mother and father are sinful. It has been millennia since we sacrificed our children to the evil idol Moloch to atone for our own sins and circumstances.

If we go outside the Scriptures, we could name thousands of spiritual leaders, writers, statesmen, musicians, composers, artists, thinkers, philosophers, playwrights, scientists, doctors, inventors, business people, and others of as much or more value who have influenced, saved or enriched our collective lives, but who came from poverty-stricken homes, were illegitimate children, had teenage mothers, had tainted parentage, were the 8th or the 18th or the 20th child born in the family, were orphaned at birth, were raised in adopted homes or orphanages, were handicapped from birth, were abused as children, were unwanted, unplanned children.

Many who fight Against Abortion and many who fight For Abortion share unfortunate heritages. But the difference is: most of us were not conceived in a time of state-sponsored and publicly-sanctioned abortion. We were allowed to live and move and have being. There was a Right To Live.

When most of us who have ever lived were born, abortion was a sin, the devil's work, an evil act done in darkness.

Somewhere, sometime, only God knows where and when, we in America and the world have lost the truth that abortion is wrong. A sinister haze has enveloped the whole area of abortion. Most of our people wander aimlessly in this miasma unable to give valid reasons for or against abortion. Others stumble on rare exceptions and then find themselves unable to make a distinction between abominable circumstances of conception and the baby who is the innocent result of the abomination.

Some, even those who have had abortions, find it difficult to affirm or to deny abortion. Most have been mentally and spiritually transported to the Land of the Lotus Eaters.

Deluded people act the way our people have been acting. People who have been raised on and surrounded by lies act like we are acting. The father of lies has been busy spinning deceit and uncertainty.

The lies and delusions which killed millions of human beings in the 1940's ended with the death, destruction and division of the nation which bred and fed those lies.

We in America must be warned. We are father and feeder of the same type of lies which have reduced certain human beings, babies in the womb, to a sub-human category which is killable.

The blood of the poor innocents is on our skirts. Jeremiah 2:34

We have lost compassion for the children of our wombs. Isaiah 49:15

We are cutting off the children from the streets. Jeremiah 9:21

We have forgotten we were once naked, squirming in our own blood. Ezekiel 16:22

"Let this be recorded for a generation yet to come, so that a people yet unborn may praise the Lord: that He looked down from His holy height, from heaven the Lord looked at the earth, to hear the groans of the

prisoners, to set free those who were doomed to die."
Psalm 102:18-20

When the Father of all life cries, "Enough!", woe to the lie-mongers! Woe to the death-dealers!
Woe, woe, America!

REDEMPTION

People who are Against Abortion are fighting a just war against those who are For Abortion. The Bible teaches us that the believer will have real enemies. Sometimes they will even be within our own homes. (Matthew 10:36) So we are not naive. We know there are wars and will be wars for us. We know we have enemies. We know we are to fight the Good Fight armed with the powerful equipment of faith and Scripture. (Ephesians 6:11-18)

In conventional wars, however, the opposing forces hate each other. We as Christian soldiers can never hate our enemies or the enemies of the Word. Our Commander teaches us to love our enemies and to pray for them.

"But I say to you, Love your enemies and pray for those who persecute you, so that you may be sons of your Father Who is in heaven." Matthew 5: 44, 45

How then can the children of God fight a war against real people who are killing real babies at the same time that they are loving and praying for them? If we love and pray for specific people, do not those very acts and emotions tend to draw us closer to them and do we not then risk condoning and forgiving the sin of abortion?

Forgiving the sin of abortion? We are forgivers! Forgiving is our definition and our distinction. What every Christian should fear is not forgiving. An unforgiving person risks being unforgiven by our Father.

"...And forgive our debts, AS we also have forgiven our debtors. Matthew 6:12

"For if you forgive men their trespasses, your heavenly Father also will forgive you; but if you do not forgive men their trespasses, neither will your Father forgive your trespasses." Matthew 6:14, 15

"And whenever you stand praying, forgive if you have anything against any one; so that your Father also Who is in heaven may forgive you your trespasses." Mark 11:25, 26

God's children should honeycomb the world with acts of forgiveness. We never "risk" forgiveness. It is our modus operandi. The ability to forgive is powerful proof of our Paternity!

Praying for and loving a doctor in your area who performs abortions will draw you closer to him. Love is action. Prayer is action. Things in the material world happen when love and prayer are put into action.

Love and prayer are not insipid non-responses to situations. That perception is from the pit and is designed to keep the battle on the terrain of flesh and blood. If we can be deceived into thinking an abortuary will shut down only if we throw man-made volleys, the battle will be lost. Walls tumble down when God's orders are followed. God has commanded us to love and to pray for our enemies and the enemies of His Word.

Picket, if you will, but pray as you picket.

Be on your knees before our God on the pavements of our land.

Pray for the owners of those aborturaries—God knows who they are. Pray that the Author of Life will cause their hearts and minds to revolt from evil. It has happened and will happen if you pray.

Pray for the doctors and nurses and receptionists who enter every day to do and to enable the deeds of death. Pray that the Life-Bringer will bring them to repentance, that He will save their souls, that He will have mercy on them who have no mercy.

Pray for the girls and women who enter those doors. Pray that the Redeemer will change their minds. Pray that He will bring them Godly counselors who will keep them from darkening those portals of death.

"For we are not contending against flesh and blood, but against the principalities, against the powers, against the world rulers of this present darkness, against the spiritual hosts of wickedness in the heavenly places." Ephesians 6:12

We must fight fire with fire. This is a spiritual battle against evil spiritual forces. The battle against abortion will be won only if we use God's weapons.

The idea of killing millions of babies in the womb obviously was hatched in the deepest rung of darkness. It is testimony to the spiritual darkness of our present age that millions of us cannot see this fact.

As we use the spiritual weapons and armament He has given us, the battle will eventually be won.

In loving and praying for all those For Abortion, we ourselves come closer to our Lord and His holiness. The closer we are to Him, the more we will hate the sin of abortion. So we will never risk losing our edge or condoning abortion by loving and praying for those in darkness.

For God hates sin, but He loves and sent His Own Son to die for the sinner. We are like our Father. On our knees and in His Word we become more and more conformed to Him Who bought us back from our own darkness.

"But God commended His love toward us in that, while we were YET sinners, Christ died for us." Romans 5:8

We hate and fight the sin of abortion, but we must love and pray for those who legislate abortions, own abortuaries, perform abortions, have abortions or actively/passively aid and abet them.

This should not be that hard for the Christian. After all, "all have sinned and come short of the glory of God." (Romans 3:23) There are only two kinds of people on this planet—saved sinners and lost sinners. We who have accepted the grace of God, who have been saved from the folly and fire of our own lives should have the most compassion for those who are still slowly burning. We know what it feels like to be lost, directionless, alone, trapped, deluded. We also know what it feels like to be listed in Romans 1:29-32:

"...filled with unrighteousness, fornication, wickedness, covetousness, maliciousness; full of envy, murder, debate, deceit, malignity; whisperers, backbiters, haters of God, despiteful, proud, boasters, inventors of evil things, disobedient to parents, without understanding, covenant breakers, without natural affection, implacable, unmerciful: who knowing the judgment of God that they which commit such things are worthy of death, not only do the same, but have pleasure in them that do them."

Our attitude toward those who are For Abortion is the same as our attitude toward the liar, the thief, the evil-doers, the pimp, the hateful, the homosexual, the lascivious, the atheist, the adulterer, the drug addict, the greedy, the boastful, the self-centered, the alcoholic, the gossip and all those who are proud they are not one of the above. We love them enough to pray for them, to go to them and to tell them they, too, can be saved.

We call them to repentance in the same way that we were called to repentance. We do not ignore the sin. We fight the sin with the sword of the Spirit which is the Word of God, but as we fight the evil which keeps them prisoner, we rescue the evil-doer in the name of and by the power of the Father Who dwells in us.

We must love the American people enough to tell them the truth. We must use the teachings of the Bible to call them to repentance as we were loved enough to be called from our sinful ways. We must not avoid the words "sin," "evil," "wicked," "immoral, "ungodly" "abomination." We must call abortion what it is and not be ashamed of the Biblical words.

It is not loving to allow our people to journey en masse down the road to perdition. It is not loving to allow our people to bump around in darkness when we have light. It is never the loving thing to withhold warning from disaster.

God loved the wicked society of Nineveh enough to send a reluctant Jonah to call them to old-fashioned repentance so they would not be destroyed by their wickedness. We are all Jonahs called by God to preach repentance and to offer forgiveness to cultures filled with evil imaginings. We may not want to do this. Jonah did not want to go to Nineveh and took an unusual journey to escape his commission. We may even want society to reap what it has so willingly and belligerently sown. We may be tempted to call down the wrath of God like a mighty sword upon the neck of sin as James and John, the Sons of Thunder, wanted the enemies of Jesus to be consumed. (Luke 9:54) But the Lord says to us what He said to James and John: "The Son of Man is not come to destroy men's lives, but to save them." (Luke 9:56)

We who abhor the sin of abortion must not be guilty of despising God's "great kindness, tolerance and patience" (Romans 2:4) toward sinners. We must go forth humbled by our own salvation, filled with forgiveness for the unsaved and armed through the Scriptures with the sure knowledge of what is right and what is wrong.

Do we fraternize with the enemy, with those For Abortion? Of course we do. How else are they to hear the Good News unless we are there speaking and living rescued lives before them?

Do we get our hands and skirts dirty? Of course we do. How else to walk in the midst of offal as our Lord did?

Do we ever fall into sin ourselves? Of course we do. Why do we need our Saviour if we are not sinners?

Does He forgive us? Of course He does and sends us back to the battle clean and chastened. We can do nothing of ourselves. He is All in All to the believer.

Will we always live missing His mark? Yes.

For we do not lift up ourselves to a wayward world. We lift Him up. We are, after all, mere servants of the Master, common stewards in His household.

To those of you, Jew or Gentile, who have not been rescued, who do not know your Father, He says:

"...as Moses lifted up the serpent in the wilderness, even so must the Son of Man be lifted up: That whosoever believeth in Him should not perish, but have eternal life. For God so loved the world, that He gave his only begotten Son, that whosoever believeth in Him should not perish, but have everlasting life. For God sent not His Son into the world to condemn the world; but that the world through Him might be saved. He that believeth on Him is not condemned: but he that believeth not is condemned already, because he hath not believed in the Name of the only begotten Son of God." John 3:14-18

The symbol of the medical profession is a snake entwined around a stick lifted up like a standard. This is the caduceus.

When the Jews were in the wilderness, a plague of venomous snakes were killing people who grumbled and moaned against God and Moses. The Jews soon realized the plague was punishment for their ungodly behavior.

They repented of their sins and begged Moses to help them. God told Moses to make a brazen serpent and lift it up on a standard among the people. Whoever would look to the brazen serpent would be saved. (Numbers 21:4-9)

Of course this crude symbol and simple act of saving faith foreshadowed a much more complex Reality Who was to be lifted up and received with the same simple act of belief.

But the symbol of the caduceus became wedded over the centuries to those who heal and has become the herald of the medical profession. It has symbolized what it originally symbolized—life, health, salvation from death. All who congregate around this standard of the medical world are to protect and to rescue. They are not to devise more advanced and efficient means of extermination.

God, the Healer, is full of mercy. He stays judgment and sends prophets to warn against the certain consequences of sin. He is unwilling that any should perish.

"The Lord is not slow about His promise as some count slowness, but is forbearing toward you, not wishing that any should perish, but that all should reach repentance." II Peter 3:9

"Or do you presume upon the riches of His kindness and forbearance and patience? Do you not know that God's kindness is meant to lead you to repentance?" Romans 2:4

"...yet when they turned and cried to Thee, Thou didst hear from heaven, and many times Thou didst deliver them according to Thy mercies. And Thou didst warn them in order to turn them back to Thy law." Nehemiah 9:28, 29

"And the Lord said (to Jonah), You pity the plant for which you did not labor, nor did you make it grow, which came into being in a night, and perished in a night. And should not I pity Nineveh, that great city, in which there are more than 120,000 persons who do not know their right hand from their left?" Jonah 4:10, 11

If you are For Abortion, the God Who gave you life and allows each breath you take implores you to flee from that wicked place. He is and has been most patient with you.

He calls you to repent while the judgment delays. He warns all those who kill the unborn to turn back to His laws.

There is nothing you or I have done, no place we have gone, no delusion so perverse, no pit so foul and deep that His Love and Mercy cannot reach us and deliver us.

He created you and me. We did not labor ourselves into life.

Our Creator is waiting for us to look to Him, high and lifted up for you and for me.

He gave us life. We are to be Life-Bearers not Death-Dealers.

Most merciful Father, I know you and I love you. I beg you to forgive me for not entering the battle Against Abortion sooner. I promise to fight for the lives of unborn babies from this day forward.

Date _____
Signed _____

Most merciful God, I have fought to legislate laws For Abortion in the courts of my country. I have aided and/or abetted laws which have killed the unborn. I repent these unlawful deeds this day _____

Signed _____

Most merciful God, I have performed abortions. I beg You to forgive me. I turn away from these deeds of death this day _____

Signed _____

Most merciful God, I own an abortion clinic. Please forgive my sins. I will close that clinic as of this day_____

Signed _____

Most merciful God, I have had an abortion. I have killed the baby growing in my womb. Please forgive me, O God. I praise You because You have heard this prayer of repentance.

Date _____

Signed _____

Most merciful Father, I have cowardly allowed the child I fathered to be aborted. I beg you to forgive this sin.

Date _____
Signed _____

Most merciful God, I have through silence and/or counsel participated in the killing of an unborn child. Forgive, I beg You, this sin.

Date _____
Signed _____

Most merciful Father, I have been involved in family planning groups which have promoted abortion. Please forgive me. I will give up my memberships and support for these groups this day.

Date _____
Signed _____

O God, I have never given my life to You Who gave me life. I confess I have not thought about You much at all. I have lived my life for myself and others. I have done many things which are wrong. I have left undone many things which I knew were right. Forgive my blindness and my folly. I accept on simple faith Your Son's death for my sins and their eternal consequences. I want to die to my self-full life and be born again into the life of Your Spirit. I accept you, Jesus, as the long-awaited Messiah, as my Saviour, Total Redeemer and Eternal King. Come into my life. I look up to You Who were lifted up for me this day

_____

Signed _____

"IF WE CONFESS OUR SINS, HE IS FAITHFUL AND JUST TO FORGIVE US OUR SINS, AND TO CLEANSE US FROM ALL UNRIGHTEOUSNESS." I JOHN 1:9

PEOPLE I WILL TALK TO ABOUT ABORTION

1.

2.

3.

4.

5.

6.

7.

PEOPLE/ORGANIZATIONS I WILL CALL ABOUT ABORTION

1. THE WHITE HOUSE: 1-202-456-1414

2.

3.

4.

5.

6.

7.

PEOPLE I WILL CALL ABOUT STEM CELL RESEARCH

1. MY OWN DOCTOR:

2. THE WHITE HOUSE: 1-202-456-1414

3.

4.

5.

6.

7.

ACTION STEPS I WILL TAKE TO STOP THE SLAUGHTER OF THE UNBORN

1. CONTRIBUTE MONEY TO A GROUP WHICH LOBBIES IN WASHINGTON AGAINST ABORTION.

2. ORGANIZE A FORUM OR DISCUSSION GROUP TO TALK ABOUT ABORTION.

3. ASK MY PRIEST, RABBI OR PASTOR WHAT HE/SHE THINKS ABOUT ABORTION.

4. INITIATE DISCUSSIONS WITH MY INTIMATES ABOUT ABORTION.

5. PASS THIS BOOK ALONG TO SOMEONE I FEEL WOULD BENEFIT FROM IT.

6. JOIN A GROUP WHICH PICKETS ABORTION CLINICS.

7. VOLUNTEER WITH AN ORGANIZATION WHICH COUNSELS WOMEN BEFORE THEY HAVE ABORTIONS OR AFTER THEY HAVE HAD ABORTIONS.

8.

9.

10.

PEOPLE I HAVE TO PRAY FOR

1.

2.

3.

4.

5.

6.

7.

OTHER BIBLE VERSES ABOUT THE SANCTITY OF LIFE

1.

2.

3.

4.

5.

6.

7.

NOTES AND QUESTIONS